THE QUILT BOOK

OF 21 POSTCARDS

Salmo trutti

SAN FRANCISCO • CALIFORNIA

Salmo trutti

P.O. BOX 280070
SAN FRANCISCO • CALIFORNIA 94128-0070

ISBN: 1-56313-875-1
TITLE #: ST875

Salmo trutti publishes a large line of photographic books and postcard books.
Please write for more information.

Printed in Korea

QUILTS
"BROKEN DIAMOND, STAR, AND LOG CABIN"

PUBLISHED BY *Salmo trutti* • SAN FRANCISCO, CALIFORNIA

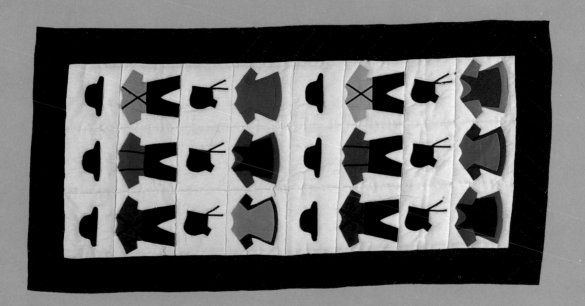

QUILTS

"AMISH BOY AND GIRL CLOTHING", CRIB QUILT

PUBLISHED BY *Salmo trutti* • SAN FRANCISCO, CALIFORNIA

QUILTS

"BALTIMORE ALBUM"

PUBLISHED BY *Salmo trutti* • SAN FRANCISCO, CALIFORNIA

QUILTS
"WEDDING RING"

PUBLISHED BY *Salmo trutti* • SAN FRANCISCO, CALIFORNIA

QUILTS
"FRUIT OF THE SPIRIT"

PUBLISHED BY *Salmo trutti* • SAN FRANCISCO, CALIFORNIA

QUILTS

"COLORADO STAR AND LOG CABIN"

PUBLISHED BY *Salmo trutti* • SAN FRANCISCO, CALIFORNIA

QUILTS

"TRIPLE BROKEN DIAMOND, STAR, AND LOG CABIN"

PUBLISHED BY _Salmo trutti_ • SAN FRANCISCO, CALIFORNIA

QUILTS
"STAR AND LOG CABIN"

PUBLISHED BY *Salmo trutti* • SAN FRANCISCO, CALIFORNIA

QUILTS

"DAHLIA"

PUBLISHED BY *Salmo trutti* • SAN FRANCISCO, CALIFORNIA

QUILTS
"LONE STAR AND LOG CABIN"

PUBLISHED BY *Salmo trutti* • SAN FRANCISCO, CALIFORNIA

QUILTS

"SUNSHINE AND SHADOW WITH DIAMOND CENTER"

PUBLISHED BY *Salmo trutti* • SAN FRANCISCO, CALIFORNIA

QUILTS
"COUNTRY LILY"

PUBLISHED BY *Salmo trutti* • SAN FRANCISCO, CALIFORNIA

QUILTS

"TRIANGLE TRIP AROUND THE WORLD"

PUBLISHED BY *Salmo trutti* • SAN FRANCISCO, CALIFORNIA

QUILTS

"SPRING FLOWER GARDEN"

PUBLISHED BY *Salmo trutti* • SAN FRANCISCO, CALIFORNIA

QUILTS
"BARN RAISING LOG CABIN"

PUBLISHED BY *Salmo trutti* • SAN FRANCISCO, CALIFORNIA

QUILTS

"LONE STAR"

PUBLISHED BY *Salmo trutti* • SAN FRANCISCO, CALIFORNIA

QUILTS

"SHADOW STAR"

PUBLISHED BY *Salmo trutti* • SAN FRANCISCO, CALIFORNIA

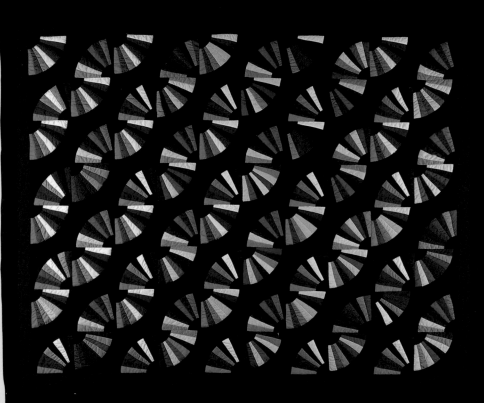

QUILTS

"GRANDMOTHER'S FAN"

PUBLISHED BY *Salmo trutti* • SAN FRANCISCO, CALIFORNIA

QUILTS
"SAMPLER"

PUBLISHED BY *Salmo trutti* • SAN FRANCISCO, CALIFORNIA

QUILTS
"THE GARDEN"

PUBLISHED BY *Salmo trutti* • SAN FRANCISCO, CALIFORNIA

QUILTS
"LOG CABIN SPLENDOR"

PUBLISHED BY *Salmo trutti* • SAN FRANCISCO, CALIFORNIA